LOCOMOTIVES

BETWEEN THE WARS

LOCOMOTIVES

BETWEEN THE WARS

Kevin Robertson

ALAN SUTTON

First published in the United Kingdom in 1991 by
Alan Sutton Publishing Ltd · Phoenix Mill · Far Thrupp · Stroud · Gloucestershire

First published in the United States of America in 1992 by
Alan Sutton Publishing Inc. · Wolfeboro Falls · NH 03896–0848

Reprinted in 1995

British Library Cataloguing in Publication Data

Robertson, Kevin
Locomotives between the wars
I. Title
385.0942

ISBN 0–86299–914–6

Library of Congress Cataloging in Publication Data applied for

Endpapers: Front 'N15' class 4–6–0 Sir Geraint *outside Eastleigh Works in 1937.*

Back: Stanier 'Jubilee' type 4–6–0 No. 5574 India *at Camden in 1935*

Typeset in Palatino 9/10.
Typesetting and origination by
Alan Sutton Publishing Limited.
Printed in Great Britain by
WBC, Bridgend, Mid Glam.

Introduction

In an age when computers and other sophisticated technology seem to dominate almost every aspect of our lives, it is difficult to equate with a time within living memory when such accoutrements were not only deemed unnecessary, but largely unheard of as well. It was an era when, on the railways at least, steam was dominant and an almost countless variety of differing engines of varying shapes and sizes could be seen at the head of trains or waiting in yards and sheds many of which have long since vanished from the scene.

Fortunately photography was already well established by the 1930s and so scenes of engines and trains are relatively common, although from the researcher's viewpoint there must always be the nagging question '. . . I wonder what was just out of camera to right (or left)?'

Previously the railways of this period have invariably been portrayed by photographs of the largest and newest engines, the majesty and performance of a Great Western 'King', LMS 'Duchess' LNER 'A4', or Southern 'Lord Nelson' seemingly of greater interest than the more humble types – even if the latter were, in fact, far more numerous. In displaying only a selection of views of large engines, the balance is incorrect, for the express engines and trains represented but a fraction of railway movement.

This volume attempts to redress such imbalance. It is an album of smaller, but equally, and some would say, more interesting-locomotive types; of everyday scenes depicting the railways as they actually were and concentrating on the locomotives themselves. After all, surely these machines are the subject of the greatest interest?

The photographs reproduced here were all taken by the late Bernard Anwell and basically fall within the parameters outlined above, with the very occasional exception for reasons of historic interest. In his capacity as a mechanical engineer, Bernard Anwell had free access to numerous railway sites nationwide and the results of that access are seen here. Following his death the collection was for some years in the hands of Walter Gilburt, himself a photographer of some note, and it is through the good offices of this individual as well as the Anwell family that this portrait is presented.

Kevin Robertson

1

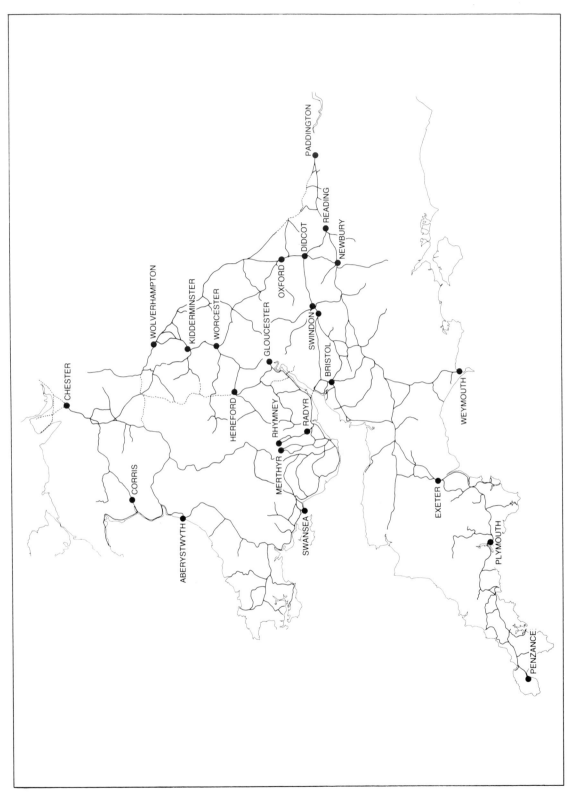

THE GREAT WESTERN

(Only locations relevant to the text are shown)

The Great Western

The 0–6–0 design for branch and other light duties remained a feature of steam operation on former GWR lines until the cessation of steam working. Although for many years this was the haunt of the 'Dean Goods', this is a later design sometimes referred to as 'Baby Castles', the '2251' engines were well-liked and common throughout the system. No. 2278 is pictured at Worcester.

28.3.37

Saddle tanks were never as common on the GWR as they were on some other lines; Swindon preferring the 'pannier' design instead, examples of which are illustrated later. Despite this a number of tank classes were originally built in this guise and a few survived into BR days. Here No. 2021, appropriately of the '2021' class is seen at Swindon awaiting Works attention and minus rods. The engine emerged from the Works in December of the same year modified with pannier tanks, in which form it survived until 1951.

27.9.36

Originally built as a tender engine, the six members of the '322' class were converted to saddle tanks at Wolverhampton Works in 1878–85. They lasted in service until the period 1921–32 and the first to be taken out of service, No. 324, can be seen at Swindon in use as a stationary boiler.

4

Seen here at Corris is 0–4–2ST No. 4. This particular engine was built by Kerr Stuart specially for the Corris Railway in 1921 and lasted until withdrawal by BR in 1948. Happily both it and its sister machine, No. 3, survive on the Talyllyn Railway.

29.6.39

Another narrow gauge line operated by the Great Western was that from Aberystwyth to Devil's Bridge, which ran three 2–6–2T engines. Seen here is former 'Cambrian' No. 1 *Edward VII*, now GWR No. 1212, at Swindon, where the Vale of Rheidol engines were taken by the GWR whenever major overhaul was required. Sadly for No. 1212 it was nearing the end of its life when this photograph was taken as it was withdrawn in December 1932 and placed on the sales list. It was scrapped shortly afterwards.

Autumn 1932

'Dukedog' No. 3215 leaving Shawford (SR) on the last leg of a journey from the Great Western via the DN&S line at Didcot. Shawford station is seen in its original form before the 'Down' relief line was extended, parallel with the train seen here. This extension took place five years after the photograph was taken.

23.3.38

The second of the two 0–4–2ST engines on the former Corris Railway, photographed at its home base of Corris. This is No. 3, built by the Falcon Engine Co. in 1878 and now running on the Talyllyn Railway as *Sir Haydn*.

June 1939

No. 2559 of the ubiquitous 'Dean Goods' class or, to be more correct, the title should be the '2301' class. No. 2559 was one of the last batch of engines built at Swindon in 1897–9 and it survived in service until October 1940. It is seen here at Wolverhampton, Oxley.

23.8.36

A number of engines, which were taken over at the time of the grouping, were later modified by the GWR with standard parts – boilers and the like. This sometimes made it difficult for the untrained eye to identify such machines. Careful examination, however, reveals No. 894 as having a non-standard cab, while the inititals GWR above the number 894 on the cab-side plate also indicate that this is an 'absorbed' engine. No. 894 is a former Cambrian Railways engine, built by Robert Stephenson & Co. in 1908 and modified by Swindon in July 1933, after which it returned to its old haunts and is seen here at Machynlleth.

June 1939

Perhaps one of the most attractive of all the small tank engine classes were those of the '517' and 'Metro' tank classes. An example of the latter is depicted here at Merthyr in the form of No. 1495. Despite appearing to be in reasonable external condition, No. 1495 was not destined to survive much longer and was withdrawn in December 1938.

5.6.38

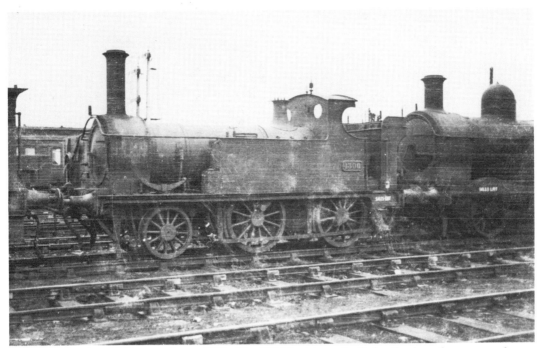

Absorbed by the GWR as early as 1876, No. 1300 had been built for the broad gauge and was originally just known by the name *Mercury*. It was converted to standard gauge in 1878 and given the number 1300 before being rebuilt in 1905 into the form shown. Withdrawn in May 1934 the engine was placed on the sales list at Swindon, but failed to attract a potential buyer and was later cut up.

Despite their old-fashioned appearance the 'Dukedog' rebuilds of 1936 onwards were a highly successful marriage of standard components and, in many cases, went on to give more than twenty years of useful service. Seen at Aberystwyth is No. 3217, now preserved, and carrying its originally intended name of *Earl of Berkeley*.

8.4.39

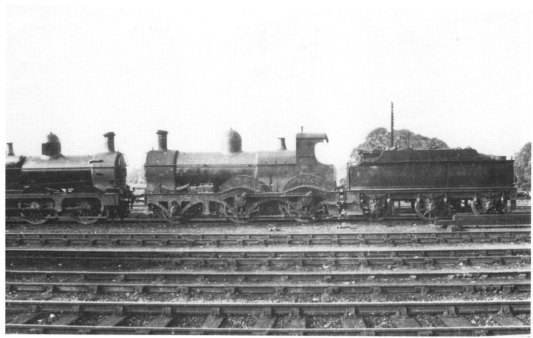

Originally in the front line of express passenger work, the 'Barnum' class of 2–4–0 engines were quickly demoted to lesser duties as train loads and speeds increased. Seen at Didcot is No. 3210; from here one of its regular duties was south towards Newbury and Winchester on the former DN&S route. No. 3210 lasted in service until March 1937.

Summer 1936

Ugly perhaps but functional, the 'Aberdare' class of outside framed 2–6–0 goods engines dated from 1900, although No. 2638, photographed at Chester, was not built until the following year. On this occasion the engine is paired with the tender from a former 'ROD' 2–8–0, which perhaps mars the otherwise neat lines of the engine profile.

June 1935

10

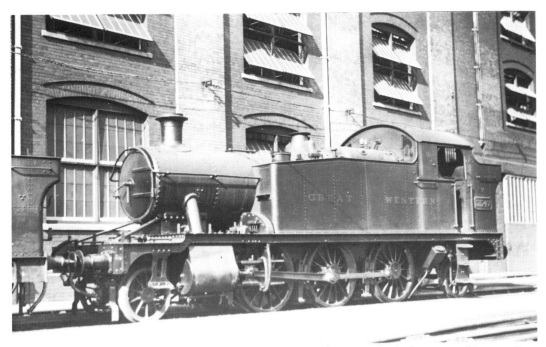

Built at Swindon in October 1928, No. 5547 is seen outside its birthplace, possibly pending overhaul. The 55xx series of tank engines were the final development of the small wheeled 'prairie' design for light branch work and they proved to be popular and capable engines, many working until the closure of the lines under BR.

September 1936

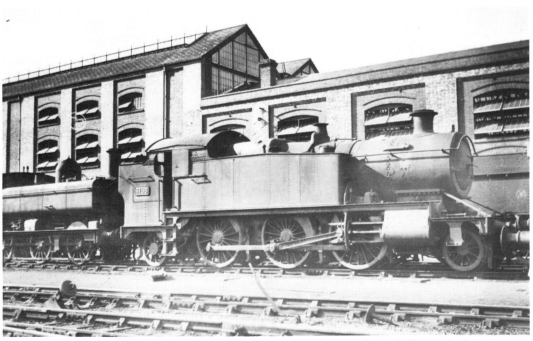

A larger wheeled 'prairie' tank, No. 3168, which was built as early as 1907. Their duties were varied and, as well as train haulage, a number were used as bankers throughout the system. No. 3168 is seen at Swindon in 1936 and it survived in service until 1950.

September 1936

Complete with telegraph pole adorning the chimney, 2–8–0 No. 5253 waits between duties at Gloucester. Primarily built for hauling coal in South Wales, the 52xx engines were quickly drafted on to goods duties elsewhere as recession in the coalfields reduced the amount of work available for them.

7.4.39

The standard GWR 0–6–2T design for South Wales, No. 6683 at Porthcawl, although unusually complete with the reporting number '124'. The 'shirt button' GWR roundal should be noted as it had been used on all new paintwork from the mid-1930s onwards.

July 1937

A number of 'absorbed' engines from the former South Wales lines were converted to Swindon style from 1923 onwards. GWR No. 34, formerly Rhymney Railway No. 17, is seen at Rhymney in June 1938. It was withdrawn in late 1949 and finally cut up in February 1950.

June 1938

Another 'absorbed' tank engine, this time No. 438 from the former Taff Vale Railway and seen at Danycraig.

18.7.37

The 0–6–2T design was popular on the railways of South Wales as witness by what is now GWR No. 240 at Radyr, formerly a Barry Railway machine. On this occasion the engine retains its original boiler and smoke box, although a GWR-style safety valve bonnet has been added.

1936

A sister engine to the one seen earlier, this is former Rhymney Railway No. 39, GWR No. 35, photographed at Radyr. It will be noted that consecutive numbers in the GWR listings did not necessarily mean consecutive numbers from former RR stock.

June 1938

A superb view of former Rhymney Railway No. 14, GWR No. 57, at Abercynon shed in 1938. This locomotive had been built for its former owners in 1911 by the firm of Hudswell Clarke and survived under BR until 1952. In the background Abercynon shed is constructed to the standard Great Western design, with offices along one side and in front the sand drier. From the number of persons visible in the background the view may well have been taken at the time of an organized shed visit.

June 1938

Formerly Taff Vale '04' class 0–6–2T No. 104 and renumbered as GWR No. 302 at Treherbert shed in 1938. Although a number of the former South Wales companies perpetuated the 0–6–2T wheel arrangement there was considerable variety over differences in detail: the firebox shape, side tank design and front sand boxes are obvious variations between engines of the Rhymney and Taff Vale systems.

June 1938

The pannier tank design 0–6–0 tank engine class was favoured by the GWR. Here an early example of the design can be seen in the form of '2021' class No. 2089 at Wolverhampton, Stafford Road in 1936. Provided only with an open-backed cab enginemen had to be hardy individuals, although some in the class were fitted with an enclosed cab in later years. No. 2089 had a life of some twenty-seven years and was withdrawn in 1951.

23.8.36

Originally Cardiff Railways No. 17, GWR No. 683, at Caerphilly in 1938. No. 17 was built by Hudswell Clarke in 1920 as an 0–6–0 saddle tank and was modified in 1926 by the GWR to the form shown here. At the time the photograph was taken the engine was clearly in need of repair as the dome cover has been removed and placed over the safety valves, so revealing the austere boiler underneath. Note also the letters GWR above the numbers on the number-plate, indicating that this was an 'absorbed' engine.

June 1938

The number of outside framed pannier tanks diminished rapidly as newer designs became available, with the survivors being banished to various out-stations for their final years of operation. One such example is shown here, No. 1629 of the '1076' or 'Buffalo' class at Swansea East Dock in July 1937. No. 1629 had been built in 1880 and had only two months left in service before being withdrawn in September 1937.

July 1937

For many years the GWR preferred inside cylinders for the majority of their smaller tank engine classes, although again the acquisition of a number of engines from 1922 onwards meant that a considerable variety of non-standard types were added to stock. Two of these came from the former Cleobury Mortimer & Ditton Priors line: No. 29 is seen in rebuilt GWR style at Kidderminster shed in March 1937. Both engines remained in the vicinity of their former owners after 1922 and later passed into BR ownership, No. 29 lasting until early 1954.

One of the last tank engine designs produced by the GWR was the 74xx series, examples of which were built at varying times between 1936 and 1950. No. 7406 dated from 1936 and is seen here in steam at Aberystwyth. Compared with the similar 64xx class engines, none of the class was fitted for auto-working.

April 1939

Former Burry Port & Gwendraeth Railway No. 13, seen here as GWR No. 2166 at Danygraig in July 1937. As can be seen, few changes had been made to the original design, although as years passed 'standard'-type boiler fittings were provided. No. 2166 dated from 1916 and remained in service until 1955.

July 1937

Outside cylindered 0–6–0PT No. 1368 on the Weymouth Harbour Tramway; the street is surprisingly devoid of traffic. In later years trains sometimes had considerable difficulty in getting through, and this was one of the reasons why tramway services were slowly reduced.

The restricted clearances and sharp curves at Weymouth Quay precluded the use of many large engine types and therefore the small shunting types so employed retained the task for a number of years. One of these is seen here, No. 2195 *Cwm Mawr*, another former Burry Port & Gwendraeth Railway machine, although now some distance from its former haunts. No. 2195 had a particularly interesting career, entering service with its former owners as their No. 5 in 1905 and renumbered by the GWR from 1922 onwards. It was withdrawn by the GWR in March 1939, only to be reinstated in that December, although this time without its former name. It then continued to work until January 1953. Notice also the bell on the framing.

Eight locomotives were 'absorbed' by the GWR from the former Llanelly & Mynydd Mawr Railway, all of which were identified by name only. GWR No. 359 *Hilda* is seen at Danygraig in July 1937, the only one of the former LMM engines to retain its name. It was by this time also fitted with a bell for dock-side working.

July 1937

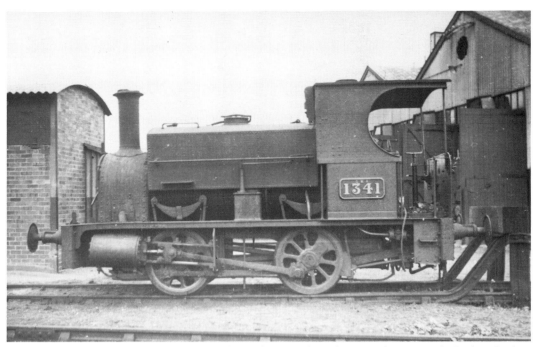

GWR No. 1341, formerly Alexander Docks Railway's *Alexandra*, seen here outside Radyr shed in 1936. Two such engines had been 'absorbed' by the GWR, and *Alexandra*, with sister engine *Trojan*, was sold out of service as early as 1932, although fortunately surviving long enough to pass into the hands of the preservationists.

1936

No. 1331 at Swindon stock shed in September 1936. The origins of this particular locomotive are unclear as records state that the number 1331 was allocated to a former Cambrian Railways engine in 1922, although this was never carried.

September 1936

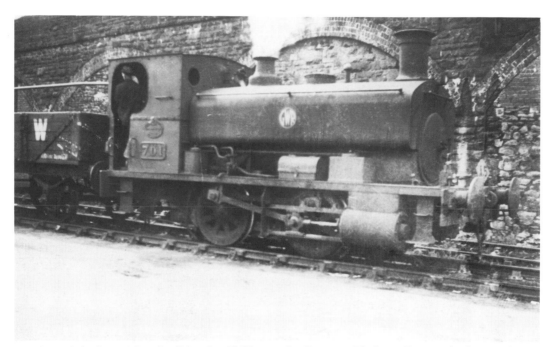

Another of the lines 'absorbed' by the GWR was the Swansea Harbour Trust, which contributed fourteen locomotives to GWR stock. GWR No. 701, formerly SHT No. 5, is seen here, although the engine was destined to be renumbered further in 1948 this time as No. 1140. It survived until May 1958.

July 1937

A variation of locomotive types and again a former SHT machine. This was SHT No. 18, dating from 1918, although seen here at Danygraig as GWR No. 1098. Again the engine was later renumbered, its final identification being No. 1145.

July 1937

Ex-Swansea Harbour Trust No. 14, GWR No. 942, at Swansea East Dock in July 1937. This engine was later renumbered No. 1142 in 1948.

July 1937

The standard GWR heavy freight design, the 28xx series, represented by No. 2873 at Worcester. The class itself dated from 1903, although No. 2873 was not completed until 1919. So successful was the class that a second batch was built some years later with only minor modifications, the last of these not entering service until as late as 1942.

1937

No look at GWR locomotives would be complete without at least a glimpse of one of the 4–6–0 types, in this case 'Saint' class No. 2980 *Coeur de Lion* at Hereford in April 1939. The engine is also attached to an 'intermediate' tender. Although already in the shadow of the later 'Castle' and 'Hall' classes, many of the 'Saints' continued to provide sterling service, No. 2980 was finally withdrawn in May 1948 after a life of some thirty-six years.

April 1939

Originally built for the Railway Operating Department to a Great Central Railway design, a number of these large 2–8–0 engines were at first loaned to, and then purchased by, the GWR from 1925 onwards. Seen at Reading, No. 3025 was acquired by the railway in June 1925 and used on heavy freight services. Despite their available power the class was not universally popular, mainly due to the knocks that developed as they became due for repair and overhaul.

GWR No. 974 at Swansea. As at Weymouth, the sharp curves and limited clearances on the dock lines necessitated the use of engines which had a short wheel-base. Of the same origins as the previous engines, this locomotive was also renumbered in 1948, this time taking the identification 1144.

1937

Approaching the conclusion the sequence on GWR locomotives, a double-headed train hard at work. 'Manor' class No. 7807 *Compton Manor* and 4–4–0 No. 3287 on the former Cambrian system sometime in 1941.

1941

One of the short-lived 4–4–2 'County' tank class to the design of Churchward. With their large diameter driving wheels and short-coupled wheelbase these engines quickly earned a reputation for rough riding and were one of the earliest of the Churchward designs to be withdrawn. Here No. 2222, is seen at an unreported location.

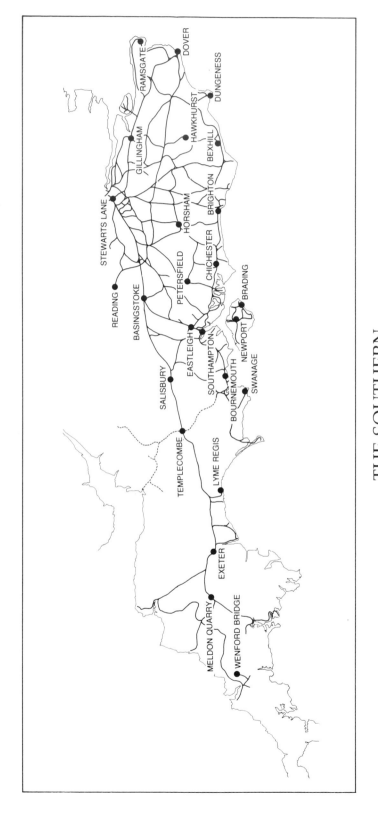

THE SOUTHERN

(Only locations relevant to the text are shown)

The Southern

As a replacement for a number of older machines, from 1923 onwards the Southern transferred a number of '02' class 0–4–4 tanks to the Isle of Wight system. This is former SR No. 218, renumbered 33 in Isle of Wight stock and named *Bembridge*. The engine is here recorded at Newport, almost immediately after its transfer from the mainland.

May 1936

Kent & East Sussex Railway No. 4, although it is pictured at Eastleigh fresh from overhaul. This particular engine was formerly SR No. 0335 but was exchanged in July 1932 for an 0–8–0 tank for which the K&ESR had little use.

1932

A panoramic view of Brighton shed, which, although undated may have been taken pre-1935 as the fourteen covered shed roads show up well. A variety of locomotive classes can be discerned including 'D' and 'E4' classes as well as what appears to be a 'C2' tender engine. In the right background is the roof of the locomotive works, while immediately behind the shed is the former Pullman car works. The main London line runs out of sight to the right of this latter building.

Crane tanks were a rarity on the Southern system; indeed, the railway possessed just two, both inherited in 1923 from the former South Eastern system. Seen here is No. 1302, formerly SER No. 302, delivered in 1891 for use at Ashford Works as well occasional duties at Folkestone Harbour and nearby. Its lifting capacity was 2½ tons. The photograph was taken at Stewarts Lane and this assists in dating the view as post-October 1938 as for ten months prior to this No. 1302 had been at the carriage works at Lancing. From 1938 No. 1302 survived on shunting duties mainly at nearby Battersea and was finally withdrawn in July 1949.

Former South Eastern Railway machine No. A225S, seen here on a low-loader and reputedly at Eastleigh. Following a varied career, which included shunting at Folkestone and Canterbury, No. A225S was employed from March 1927 at Meldon Quarry, Okehampton, although in 1938 a firebox inspection revealed repairs were required and the engine was duly despatched to Eastleigh for repair in the manner seen. Unfortunately, closer examination revealed wasting of the frames had also occurred and it was withdrawn shortly after the photograph was taken.

March 1938

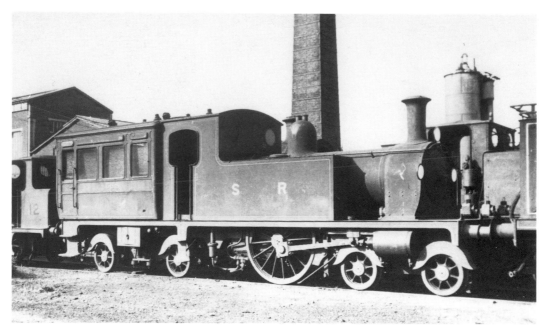

Drummond's 'Bug', photographed during its last days at Eastleigh. Built in 1899 primarily for use as a mobile inspection vehicle by the then Chief Mechanical Engineer, Dugald Drummond, the sight of this vehicle approaching was guaranteed to send chill shivers down the spines of the staff. Following Drummond's retirement in 1912 the vehicle was little used, indeed its main activity appears to have been taking VIPs on tours of the newly completed works at Southampton Docks. Finally withdrawn in August 1940, the carriage portion survived at first as a hut at Eastleigh Carriage Works, but it was later rescued for preservation and is now slowly being restored to its former glory at a narrow gauge site in south Hampshire.

13.5.40

Motor fitted 'M7' tank No. 129 at Eastleigh. Besides the original vacuum brake equipment provided when new, the engine has provision for air brakes – hence the pump, this time on the side of the smokebox.

August 1935

An unusual and rare view of SR No. 753 at Waterloo, an electric locomotive from 'The Drain' – the former LSWR underground line between Waterloo and Bank.

June 1938

Former Southampton Dock Co. 0–4–0ST No. 3458 *Ironside* at Eastleigh. Built by Hawthorn Leslie & Co. in 1890 it became LSWR No. 458 in March 1901 assuming the number shown in 1912. The engine remained in service until June 1954.

Some of the best known of all the engine types used for shunting at Southampton Docks were the 'B4' tank engines, a number of which were for many years referred to by name only. This is what was officially No. 176, although sporting the name *Guernsey* and again seen at Eastleigh. The engine was built in 1893 and lasted until 1948.

All of the '02' tank engines working on the Isle of Wight were gradually given enlarged coal bunkers; this feature showing up well on No. 32 *Bonchurch* at Newport. This particular engine had arrived from the mainland in May 1928 and was formerly numbered No. 226. The engine remained in service until late 1964.

1936

In July 1932 three former LBSCR 'E1' tank engines were transferred to the Isle of Wight. Seen here is No. 2 *Yarmouth* photographed at Newport. Never as numerous on the island as the '02' class, the four engines of the 'E1' type based on the system performed sterling service, often working coal trains from Medina Wharf near Cowes. No. 2 lasted in service until September 1956.

July 1932

'Terrier' tank No. W9 at Brading with a Bembridge branch train. Today little remains of the multitude of trackwork depicted in the photograph; the railway now consists of just a single, electrified line, as part of the route from Ryde to Shanklin.

No. W2 *Yarmouth* at Newport, Isle of Wight. Compare the size of this engine with that of the 'Terrier' just visible behind.

24.5.36

Taken on the picturesque Wenford Bridge branch in Cornwall, one of the SR's most far flung outposts. Beattie 'Well Tank' No. 3314 pauses in its duties with a mineral train. Note, the chimney is missing on the negative!

5.7.38

An ex-SECR '01' class 0–6–0, SR No. 1044, seen at Ramsgate in December 1936. This particular engine dated from 1898 and was rebuilt in the form shown in 1912. Following an undistinguished career it lasted in service until June 1951.

December 1936

The SECR had little need for large freight locomotives as, apart from coal from the Kent coalfields, its goods traffic was limited. Therefore, a locomotive with 0–6–0 wheel arrangement was sufficient and this was then also suitable for other duties should this be required. Here one of the highly successful 'C' class of engines, No. 1068, can be seen at Hither Green in 1937. The class eventually totalled 109 machines, all except two passing into BR ownership.

1937

For front line passenger duties the SECR built the 'D' class 4–4–0 engines, which were first introduced in 1903. For many years they performed admirably, working the heavy boat and Kent-coast trains over the difficult route to and from London. Heavier trains and ever increasing schedules meant that they were eventually superseded by newer engines, although many remained at work on passenger relief duties well into the 1950s. Seen here is SR No. 1075 at Gillingham shed.

November 1938

More commonly known as 'Small Hoppers' this is Dugald Drummond design 'K10' 4–4–0 No. 150 at Eastleigh. Ideally suited to light freight and semi-fast passenger duties, the class was a common sight on many former LSWR lines. However, as a result of new construction their numbers dwindled rapidly; the first being disposed of in January 1947. No. 150 lasted until February 1948, while the last of the forty strong class was gone by the end of August 1951.

March 1938

For many years it was the practice of the LBSCR to name most of its engines; 'B4X' No. 2049 was formerly identified as No. 49 *Queensland*. Built in 1901, the engine is seen here in its last days at Eastleigh. It was withdrawn the following month.

December 1935

Out to grass at Eastleigh, Drummond 'D15' No. 463 in the siding that later flanked the end of the runway at the nearby airport.

Former 'Brighton Terrier' tank, numbered as service engine 515S, was originally LBSCR No. 50 *Whitechapel*, later becoming their No. 650. It was later renumbered 9 and named *Fishbourne*. Not surprisingly, it saw service on the Isle of Wight before its penultimate change to that seen here. The engine was finally identified as BR No. 32650 and lasted until 1963.

Representing the Adam's design '395' class is SR No. 3083 seen at Eastleigh. This engine was one of three of the class which was fitted with a former 'Kirtley' boiler from Ashford and it lasted until withdrawn in 1953.

February 1939

Entering service in 1887 it is not surprising that the Adam's 'A12' class became known as the 'Jubilees' and were at first employed on fast services on both the Bournemouth and West of England main lines from Waterloo. By the time this photograph was taken No. 618 was already well past its prime, a number of sister engines from the class having already been scrapped. No. 618 lasted until January 1948.

1936

Arguably one of the best proportioned of all express types from the late-Victorian era were the 'X6' class of 1895/6. Designed for fast express duties, they must have cut a dashing sight in gleaming LSWR livery – a far cry from the drab SR paintwork displayed here by No. 660 at Eastleigh. At the time the photograph was taken No. 660 had already been withdrawn, although five of the original ten members of the class still survived, No. 658 lasting until December 1946.

1937

Slightly smaller and pre-dating the 'X6' design were the twenty engines of the 'X2' class. No. 592 is seen broadside on at Eastleigh awaiting the cutter's torch.

1937

An impressive ground level view of 'D15' class 4–4–0 No. 463 at Eastleigh. Originally provided with an 8-wheeled tender, the 6-wheeled version photographed here was fitted in early 1926 and was probably retained for the rest of the engine's life. Originally employed on the heaviest trains, the class was one of the successes of their designer, Dugald Drummond, lasting in service for some forty years and only ceasing work in the early 1950s.

1937

Compared with the other lines south of the Thames the LBSCR made extensive use of tank engines for fast passenger work, with the 'I3' class being introduced from 1907 onwards. Despite their success they were rapidly replaced on the fastest trains by larger engines, although they continued to give stirling service for many years. The class of twenty-seven remained intact until 1944, when No. 2024 was the first to be withdrawn having completed a total distance of just over 1.1 million miles. The last in the class survived until May 1952.

Similar in appearance to the 'Terrier' tanks, but having the 0–4–2T wheel arrangement, No. 216 is a former LBSCR 'D1X' class engine which differs from the standard 'D1' engine by reason of the larger boiler mounted high on the frame. The machine is depicted in store at an unknown location.

Former LBSCR No. 363 *Goldsmaid*, seen here devoid of name and running as SR No. 2363 at Bexhill West. Built at Brighton as the first of the class in June 1892, the engine ran a total of 1,457,909 miles before being withdrawn just prior to nationalization.

Formerly 'E1' class 0–6–0T, No. 2096 was one of ten engines of the class rebuilt as an 'E1R' from 1927 onwards. The conversion work involved increasing both water and coal capacities and as a result a pony truck was also supplied. In addition a new cab of SECR design was fitted. The result was an efficient, if somewhat visually unpleasing machine. All of the conversions survived into BR days, No. 2096 lasting until November 1956.

Photographed at New Cross Gate is 'E1' No. 2142, fitted with a Westinghouse air pump on the cab side.

May 1937

'D1' No. 2226 and 'E1' 2690 at Brighton on an unreported date. The 'D1' was destined to be withdrawn before nationalization, although her sister engine would survive well into BR days.

'T1' class 0–4–4T No. 15 at Eastleigh in 1939 displaying a headcode for a Southampton to Andover service. In the background it is possible to discern a coal stack; these were laid down as insurance against any difficulty in securing supplies. This engine was built in 1895 and withdrawn in 1944. Although several of the class survived into BR ownership, all had gone by the summer of 1951.

1939

Arguably one of the most elegant of all tank engine classes, the Adam's design '415' class was originally built for the London suburban services, but electrification made them redundant and they transferred to branch line duties on the former LSWR system. Apart from three, all had gone by the end of 1927. No. 3520 was one of two kept for working the Lyme Regis branch where their radial rear axle proved to be ideal on such a sharply curved line. The engine is seen at Lyme Regis; it lasted until 1961 having continued in service for seventy-six years. Happily one of the class survives and is at present on the Bluebell Line in Sussex.

1938

'E4X' class No. 2478 shown at Norwood depot. A number of these engines were rebuilt by Marsh from the original Billington 'E4' design, although engines of the original type survived well into BR days.

1938

The unique SR No. 949, formerly the Kent & East Sussex Railway *Hecate*. This engine was acquired by the Southern in July 1932. From this time on it performed a variety of shunting roles at varying locations and was affectionately known by its crews as 'Old Hiccups' because of the faltering exhaust sound when running under easy steam. It lasted until March 1950.

1932

Intended as a design for yard shunting, the 'G6' class first entered service in 1894, although No. 276 seen here was a slightly later engine dating from 1900. It is photographed here in typical role at Eastleigh.

February 1937

The 4–4–2 'Atlantic' type of wheel arrangement was popular on a number of railways in late-Victorian and Edwardian times and the LBSCR built two classes, 'H1' and 'H2' types, from 1905 onwards. 'H1' No. 2040 *St Catherine's Point* is seen here at Eastleigh in 1939 and is in remarkably good external condition. Unfortunately, even at this time the days of the class were numbered and the engine was withdrawn in 1944.

1939

Former SECR 'H' class 0–4–4T No. 1295 at Ramsgate in 1936. First introduced in 1905, this numerous class gave stirling service both on the lines of its original owners and later on varying parts of the Southern system. With the exception of two, all sixty-six members of the class passed into BR ownership, with the last working until the start of 1964.

1936

A former LBSCR 'I2' 4–4–2 No. 19 seen here as War Department No. 72401 at Brighton. Although allocated the name *Kingsley* it is thought that the plates were never carried. As SR No. 2019 the engine had been withdrawn in November 1937 and placed in store until, with a sister machine, it was towed to Bournemouth for use as a temporary air-raid shelter. They were then purchased by the War Department in 1942 and worked passenger services on the Longmoor Military Railway until withdrawn again in 1946 and finally cut up in 1951.

1941

Awaiting the cutter's torch at Eastleigh in August 1935 is former 'I2' class 4–4–2T No. 2012. A former LBSCR engine, it had a life of just twenty-seven years from the time of building in 1908.

August 1935

'R' class 0–6–0, No. 1070 at Reading (SR) in 1938. This was one of a number of this class provided with a Stirling type of round top cab intended to allow it to work the limited clearance of the Canterbury–Whitstable route. The engine survived until 1942.

1938

One of the big and beautifully proportioned 'W' class tanks, No. 1923 seen here at Hither Green. Although eminently suitable for passenger working, the class was rarely, if ever, seen on such duties – a throwback to 1927 when a large tank of the 'K' class was derailed at the head of a passenger service, resulting in considerable loss of life.

March 1937

'Rememberance' class 4–6–0 No. 2332 *Stroudley* at Eastleigh. Originally built as 4–6–4 tank engines, the seven members of the class were all rebuilt in the form seen between 1934–6. A number were also loaned to the GWR for work shortly after the photograph was taken and, according to ex-GWR man Harold Gasson, acquitted themselves well.

1941

Obviously in the course of receiving Works attention, 'N15' class 4–6–0 *Sir Geraint* stands outside the front of Eastleigh Works in 1937. At first glance it appears as if the engine has been involved in a front end collision, although closer examination reveals that part of the framework is missing to allow ease of access to the valves and steam chest.

1937

One of the highly-acclaimed 'Schools' class of engine, No. 937 *Cranleigh*, photographed at Eastleigh in May 1939. The engine is sporting one of the ugly Bulleid wide chimneys, and while this possibly improved steaming – although this is questionable – it certainly did nothing to enhance the aesthetic appeal. The headcode is of particular interest and as the engine is in steam it can only be taken to imply a special working.

May 1939

Another of the splendid 'Schools' class 4-4-0s, represented here by No. 906 *Sherborne* at Eastleigh. This machine is in near original condition, with the small chimney and six-wheeled tender. All the class were built with inwardly sloping cab sides and tender raves – for clearance purposes when working through the narrow tunnels on the Hastings line.

1941

The largest of the Maunsell design engines were the sixteen members of the 'Lord Nelson' class represented here by No. 862 *Lord Collingwood*. As with the engines belonging to other companies, many of the Southern types portrayed an outline 'family' style: the cab and smoke deflectors design being standardized on a variety of classes.

1939

The LSWR had introduced the 4–6–0 'S15' class for working heavy freight duties in 1920 and these proved to be capable and strong engines. For many years their main tasks involved working between the London yards and either Southampton Docks or towards the West Country. No. 507 is seen in Eastleigh Works yard.

August 1937

A variety of Southern types await their next tour of duty at Bournemouth shed. Bournemouth was responsible for supplying motive power for a variety of duties including trains to and from Weymouth and Southampton as well as the 'old' line via Ringwood and the branches to Lymington and Swanage.

Brand new, 'Q' class 0–6–0 No. 533 at Eastleigh, with the cab side window blanked off as a war-time precaution. This was the last of Maunsell's designs for the SR and, although lacking any obvious modern features, nevertheless they were engines which performed well on goods and other medium weight trains.

January 1941

A new 'Q' class 0–6–0 No. 532 outside the front of Eastleigh shed in 1938 awaiting a running in turn. The twenty members of the class were the last to be designed by Maunsell prior to his retirement and were conventional yet successful machines. The engine is sporting a livery of unlined black.

1938

The SR used 'S15' class 4–6–0s for heavy freight duties, although such was their flexibility that it was not unknown for these to be pressed into service on passenger workings during summer weekends. No. 834, apparently after overhaul at Eastleigh.

1941

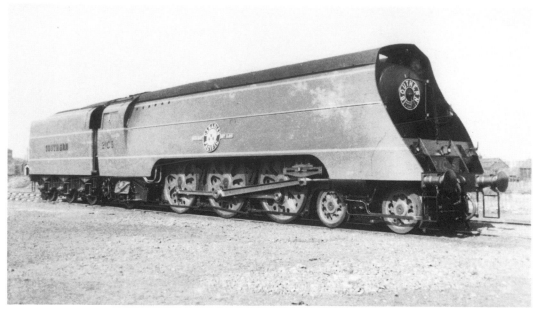

Fifth of the batch of 'Merchant Navy' engines was No. 21C5 *Canadian Pacific,* seen at Eastleigh. Already a number of modifications can be seen to have been made, including the circular plate on the smoke box door as well as a ribbed line along the casing. This latter feature was due to the use of a lightweight boarding instead of the heavy metal plates previously provided for the side sheeting.

Brand new 'Merchant Navy' class 4–6–0 No. 21C1 at Eastleigh. Intended as nothing other than an express passenger design, Bulleid was able to push through his new engines on the basis that they could be used for mixed traffic and, indeed, some of their first work was on heavy freight trains between Salisbury and Exeter. The heavy cast plate on the tender proclaiming ownership is worthy of note. The view makes an interesting comparison with that of the model mock-up seen on p. 63.

18.3.41

A head-on view of 21C1 'Channel Packet' at Eastleigh in 1941. On the smoke box is the original design Southern plate, which was later altered as it was felt that an inverted horseshoe would bring bad luck.

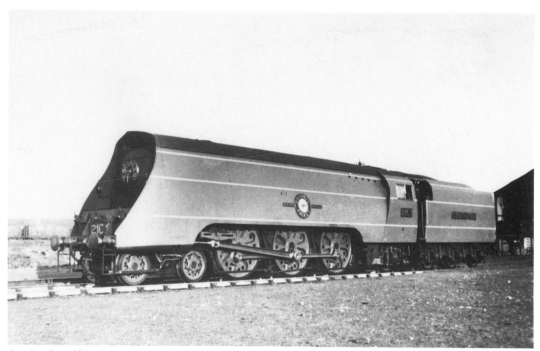

A mixed traffic or express passenger engine? Such was the discussion at the time 21C1 emerged from Eastleigh.

Seen from the rear three-quarter angle the massive proportions of the new engine are apparent, although the telegraph pole between cab and tender was not part of the original Bulleid design!

A foretaste for the Southern of things to come. A photograph of the mock-up for the Bulleid 'Merchant Navy' class, which was destined to appear the following year. Compared with previous Southern designs the class was nothing short of revolutionary and they remain, perhaps, one of the most talked about locomotive designs.

1940

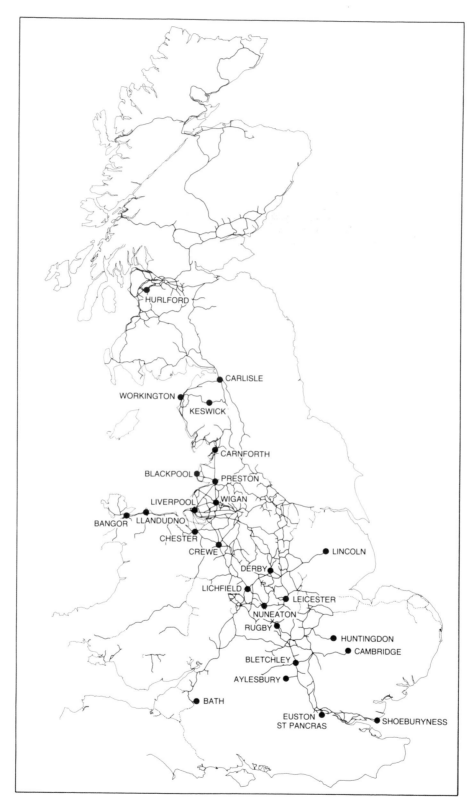

THE LONDON, MIDLAND & SCOTTISH
(Only locations relevant to the text are shown)

The London, Midland & Scottish

A 4–4–0 dating back to Midland days and represented by LMS No. 727 at Kentish Town. Introduced as far back as 1901 several of the class survived until 1948, although not so the engine shown here.

1937

One of the massive 2–6–6–2T Beyer-Garratt locomotives. Built by Beyer-Peacock from 1927 onwards, thirty-three passed into BR ownership. Despite their massive bulk, they were never regarded as the equal of later designs, notably the BR '9F' class, and all were scrapped by 1958. The Beyer-Garratt design was never popular on UK railways, although large numbers were built by British manufacturers and successfully worked a number of railway systems in other parts of the world.

Former L&Y 0–4–0T No. 11202 at Derby. Apart from works' shunting, a number of the class were stationed at Liverpool for working through the docks and streets. It was for this purpose that these engines were fitted with a crude plate – serving as a spark arrester, on top of the chimney.

1938

2–4–0 No. 20008 at Crewe South. Perpetuating a design dating back to the late 1850s, the engine was already on borrowed time and was scrapped long before nationalization.

Spring 1935

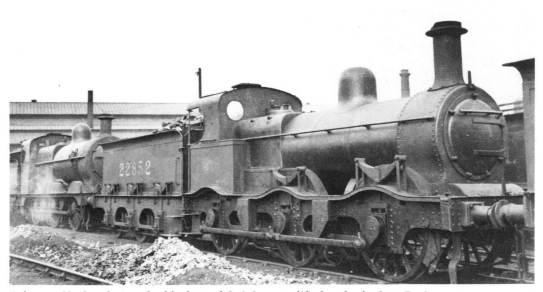

A former Kirtley design double-framed 0–6–0 as modified and rebuilt at Derby and seen here at Saltley in March 1935. For many years the former Midland Railway had continued a 'small engine policy' and this was a classic example of the type of machine which remained in use far longer than its counterparts on other systems.

March 1935

Johnson design 2–4–0 No. 211, photographed at Carnforth on an unreported date. Built in 1880, the last of the class survived until 1938, with a number of engines being reboilered with a Belpaire firebox. Judging by the sackcloth on the chimney and safety valve bonnet, No. 211 is clearly in store.

An ex-Johnson, Midland Railway, design 0–6–0, No. 3243 at Kentish Town. The fireman appears to be in the process of either mounting or dismounting, a position often occupied by shunters while engines were working in yards and sidings.

June 1937

Former Lancashire & Yorkshire 0–6–0 No. 135, although photographed here as LMS No. 12404 at Wigan Central. Originally classified as '11' class, the engine was built at Horwich in 1900 and survived until 1953.

1936

Midland Railway 'Standard' class '2' goods engine as LMS No. 3171 at Derby in 1938. Clearly this was photographed after overhaul. A number of the class had long lives and survived past nationalization.

1938

Another 'Standard' class '2', this time No. 3564 at Toton in 1935. In the background can be seen the tall coaling plant, which was a feature at a number of LMS engine sheds.

1935

LMS designed and built '2P' No. 653 at Llandudno in 1935. Similar in appearance to a number of other 4–4–0 types, the class was fitted with 6 ft 9 in driving wheels. Of interest is the feed-water heater alongside the smoke-box.

One of the most famous of all Midland types was the 4–4–0 compound design, introduced in 1905. The outside cylinders were of conventional high pressure steam type, while inside the frames there was a single low pressure cylinder. Provided that they were treated with respect when starting, the engines performed well with many lasting into BR service. Despite this the compound design was never as popular in Britain as elsewhere – particularly Europe. Engine No. 1043 was photographed at Kentish Town.

Winter 1935/6

Nearly six hundred of the 'Standard' LMS '4F' class were introduced from 1924. Basically a Midland design, the class worked all over the former LMS system and were to be seen mainly on goods services. No. 4565, apparently attached to passenger stock is seen at Derby.

June 1938

Another '4F', this time No. 4529 at Cricklewood.

1935

Ex-Glasgow & South Western 0–6–0 No. 376, pictured here as LMS No. 17188. This engine was completed in 1900 and then rebuilt by Vickers & Co., Barrow in 1920. It survived in service until April 1937.

One of the principal constituents of the LMS group was the former London & North Western system from whom the LMS acquired a variety of large passenger classes. Included among these were the 4–6–0 Bowen-Cooke design 'Sir Gilbert Claughton' class, which were classified in power group '5'. Seen here is No. 5975 *Talisman* at Camden shed.

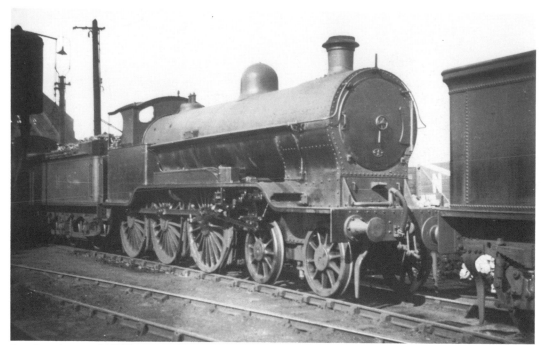

Another former LNWR type, this time 'Prince of Wales' class 4–6–0 No. 25726 photographed at Crewe Works. A number of the class carried names, although those towards the end of the batch, of which No. 25726 was one, were not so adorned.

Former LNWR No. 25673 *Lusitania* at Rugby. Dating back to a design first introduced in 1911, the engines of the 'Prince of Wales' class had already been eclipsed from front line passenger duty and few survived to BR in 1948.

1938

4–6–0 No. 8830 of the Whale '19 Goods' class, photographed at Crewe Works. This class was given power classification '4'.

1936

Another of the same class, this time No. 8818 in Bangor shed in 1935. From the look of the front framing the engine had only recently had its smoke box cleaned and some ash can be seen ready to be cleaned off before disposal is complete. Notice also the fire-irons leaning up against the shed wall – very unwieldy items to handle.

1935

In later years the LNWR named most of its passenger engines. LMS No. 5364, formerly LNWR No. 1623, carried the name *Nubian*. Seen at Chester, the engine is of the famous 'George V' class, of which ninety engines were built between 1910 and 1915. Thirty-seven were still in existence in 1934 and were renumbered by the LMS with 20,000 added to their numbers. Only two survived into BR ownership.

In the last few months of peace, 'George V' class 4–4–0 No. 25371 *Moor Hen* waits between duties at Llandudno Junction on 25 June 1939. Notice again the superbly built coal stack alongside the engine, which required considerable skill to erect. From time to time the coal would have to be rotated and burnt and replaced by fresh stocks to prevent supplies from becoming 'stale'.

25.6.39

Dating back to a Webb design of 1892, this is 0–8–0 No. 8952 of class '62a' at Bescot shed. Compared with similar aged passenger types a large number of this class of goods engine survived well into BR days, working alongside more modern types such as the LMS '8F' and BR '9F' designs.

0–6–0 saddle tank No. 7435 at Llandudno Junction in 1935. A large number of this class passed to the LMS, although the numbers rapidly diminished in the following years.

1935

Awaiting its next turn of duty in a line-up of other engines at Carlisle Kingmoor, is LMS 0–6–0 No. 17594.

An unidentified former Lancashire & Yorkshire 0–4–4 in use as a stationary boiler at Blackpool North. This was by no means an uncommon end for a number of engines. A 'shore' supply of water was laid on for the injectors, while steam-raising was in the hands of a single fireman.

Ex-L&Y 2–4–2T No. 10648 leaving Wigan Central. Nearly two hundred of this class of engine were taken over by the LMS, the design being instantly recognizable by the short bunker.

1934

Another member of the same class, this time seen broadside at Southport. The 2–4–2T wheel arrangement was used by a number of the pre-grouping railway companies, although its days were numbered as train weights and speeds increased. The final development of the type was the large 2–6–4T classes of the LMS and BR.

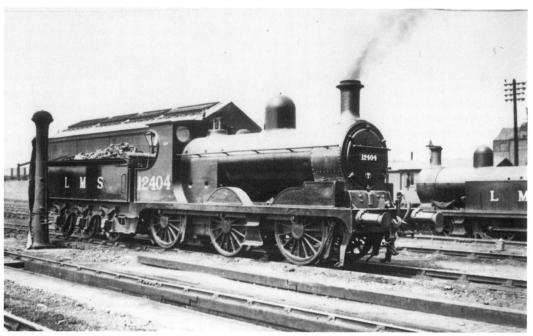

One of the numerous Aspinall '27' class engines, of which over three hundred were built. This is No. 12404 seen at Wigan Central and in remarkably clean external livery.

Webb 0–6–2 'coal tank' No. 7806 at Crewe Works. Fitted with the distinctive design driving wheels and spokes of the period, No. 7806 is clearly awaiting attention as its coupling rods have been removed.

Former Webb design *Cauliflower* 0–6–0 No. 8518 at Keswick station. Today, little remains of the railway at this point, although in the vicinity of the station at least it has been turned into a pleasant country walk.

1937

One of the big LNWR 4–4–2 'Precursor' tank engines, No. 6818 at Crewe Works. Basically a tank engine version of the 4–4–0 'Precursor' class, fifty examples of this tank engine class were built. None have survived into preservation.

Seen running as LMS No. 7883, this is a former LNWR 0–8–2 tank of Bowen-Cooke design, pictured outside Liverpool–Speke shed. Notice the two solid spokes to each driving wheel provided for 'balance' purposes.

Largest of all the LNWR tank classes was the inside cylinder 4–6–2T 'Prince of Wales' tank class. This is No. 6964 seen at Bangor. As the name implies, this was a variant of the 4–6–0 'Prince of Wales' class, although unlike their tender engine counterparts, the tank engines were not named.
1935

An unusual British design, the square saddle tank, seen here on a Webb design 0–6–0T No. 27475 at Birkenhead North. Hardly appealing to the eye such a variant was rare.

This time a former LNWR engine in the form of No. 27512, an 0–6–0T to the design of Park. Classified from 1928 as '2F' class, the engine is seen outside the shed at Bow.

1935

A former North London Railway 0–4–2 crane tank, No. 2721, photographed at Bow. A number of these engines survived nationalization, carrying numbers in the 58xxx series.

1939

An ex-Lancashire & Yorkshire 0–6–0ST at Bletchley in 1938, although regretfully records fail to reveal the number of the engine.

1938

Furness Railway design 0–6–2T No. 11636 at an unreported location.

1938

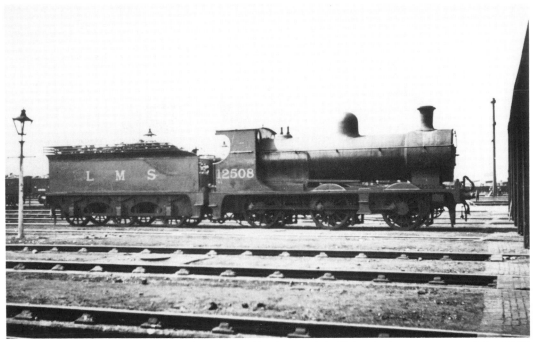

Another Furness Railway type, this time a Pettigrew 4 ft 7½ in design, represented by LMS No. 12508 outside Workington shed.

Fitted with a long coal bunker, this is ex-L&Y, Aspinall-Hughes design 2–4–2T No. 10866 at Wigan Central in 1936. In the background is its sister engine No. 10678, although this has the short rear bunker design; both machines seem well-stocked with good quality coal.

1936

Taken at Hurlford on the former Glasgow & South Western system, this is 0–6–2T No. 16900.
June 1936

The Caledonian Railway built a number of 4–6–0 passenger engines towards the end of its independent existence, and the LMS perpetuated some of these designs for a short time afterwards. Seen here is No. 14644, of the Pickersgill '60' class, which despite their size were only rated as classification '4P'. The photograph was taken at Carlisle Kingmoor.

Believed to be LMS No. 169, this is another ex-Scottish Railways machine, although unusually neither the date nor location of the photograph are reported.

An example of the delightful little L&Y 'pugs'. No. 11202 seen at Derby in 1938. Fitted with dumb buffers, members of the class were scattered throughout the LMS system and were primarily used for works, collieries and dock shunting.

1938

Webb 5 ft 6 in design 2–4–2T No. 6704 at Bletchley. Intended for passenger service, over one hundred and fifty of the class were at one time in service, but none passed into BR ownership.
1938

Another crane tank, this time No. 3248 seen at Crewe Works.
1936

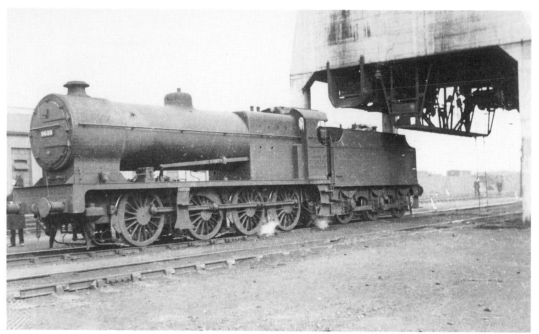

No. 9630, a big 0–8–0 Fowler design for the LMS, photographed under the coal hopper at Cricklewood, London. Despite being built from 1929 onwards, their parentage can clearly be discerned as being Midland influenced, although they put paid once and for all to the former Midland Railway small engine policy.

Designed by Sir Henry Fowler and introduced from 1929 onwards, this 0–8–0 goods engine showed considerable Midland influence, particularly the boiler, cab and tender. One hundred and seventy-five of the class were built in the number series 9600–9674. The penultimate member of the class, No. 9673, is seen here at Toton in 1935, equipped with a rather unsightly feed-water heater.

1935

The L&Y possessed a number of 4–6–0 classes, which were then inherited by the LMS. Unfortunately, it became the practice to only identify these by small cabside numerals and consequently the number of this example photographed at Preston is not reported.

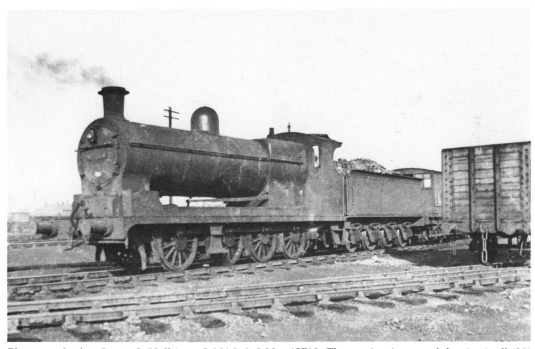

Photographed at Lostock Hall is ex-L&Y 0–8–0 No. 12710. The engine is one of the Aspinall '30' class fitted with a small boiler. Two other variations were also built, one as a compound engine and the other running as a simple expansion machine, but equipped with a larger boiler. All came under power group '6'.

Built to the Stanier '8F' design, this is WD No. 591 at Eastleigh. In November 1941 the locomotive was despatched to Persia to become their No. 41.229 before returning to War Department use as No. 70591. It finally became BR No. 48016.

c. 1941

As Chief Mechanical Engineer of the LMS, Sir William Stanier introduced a number of large tank engine classes. This is his 3-cylinder 2–6–4T design dating from 1934, thirty-seven of which were built. The doyen of the class, No. 2500, is seen on a passenger train at Camden.

1935

Another class introduced from 1934 onwards was the Stanier 'Jubilee' type, a 3-cylinder 4–6–0 with large 6 ft 9 in driving wheels. They were widely used on all but the heaviest and fastest trains, with nearly two hundred eventually running. All were named and here No. 5574 *India* is seen in striking crimson-lake livery at Camden.

1935

Forerunner of the famous 'Black 5' class were the Stanier 'Mogul' engines introduced in 1933/4. A number of features were common to all the Stanier classes including the cab design, taper boiler and top feed, all of which can clearly be seen on No. 2950 photographed at Crewe South.

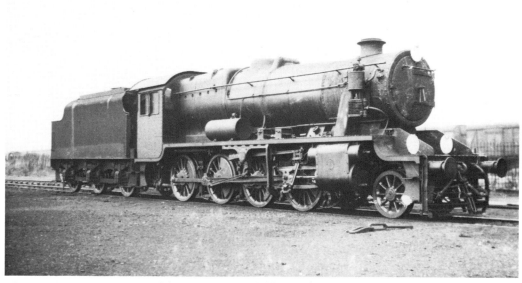

A Stanier design '8F' equipped for war service. A Westinghouse pump and air reservoir have been added.

To conclude the section on LMS steam types is another 4–6–0. Based on the earlier 'Royal Scot' design, the slightly smaller 'Patriot' class of 1930–4 worked on similar duties to the 'Jubilee' class, yet, with their parallel boiler and smoke deflectors, presented a totally different appearance. No. 5534 *E. Tootal Broadhurst* is seen at Kentish Town depot in June 1937.

June 1937

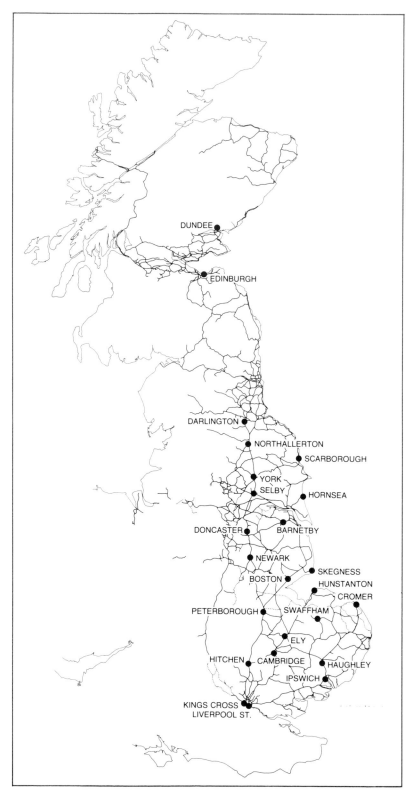

THE LONDON & NORTH EASTERN
(Only locations relevant to the text are shown)

96

The London & North Eastern

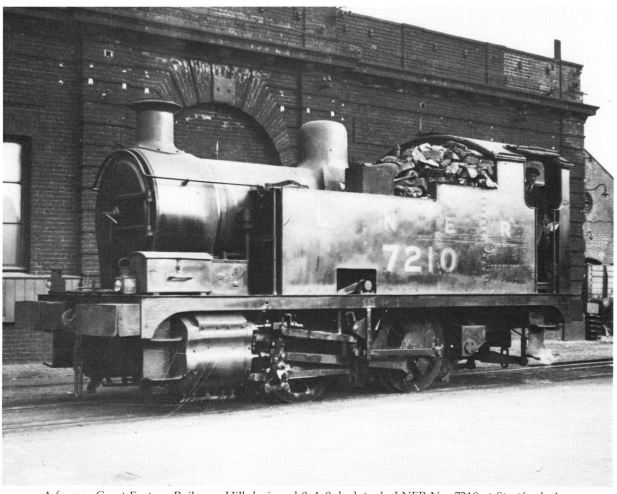

A former Great Eastern Railway, Hill designed 0–4–0 dock tank, LNER No. 7210 at Stratford. As with similar LMS engines, the use of dumb buffers and link couplings will be noted, while No. 7210 has evidently just been coaled judging by the mound on top of the side tanks.

March 1938

One of the large ex-Metropolitan Railway 2–6–4 tanks designed by Hally in 1925. This impressive design had a number of similarities to the large tank engine classes designed by Maunsell for the SECR and SR, although on the LNER the design was not as popular and the two members of the class that survived nationalization were taken out of service in 1948 without receiving their new numbers. LNER No. 6161 is seen at Stratford.

1938

LNER 4–4–4T No. 6418 at Stratford. This type of wheel arrangement was not popular with locomotive designers for, although it allowed for a considerable amount of forward and rearward bogie movement, there was also considerable loss of adhesive weight. Not surprisingly then, later tank engine designs were either of the 2–6–2 or 2–6–4 type.

12.3.38

A delightfully clean 0–6–0 No. 069 at Stratford.

March 1938

The former Great Central Railway possessed a number of large tank engine classes. This was originally a '1B' class, the first 2–6–4T design in the country. Despite such a pedigree they were not a particularly successful machine and somewhat unkindly earned the nickname of 'crabs'. Seen here is former GCR No. 340 at Neasden, although pictured as LNER No. 5340. It was later renumbered 9059 in June 1946 and allocated BR No. 69059, although it was withdrawn in August 1949 without having carried the latter identification.

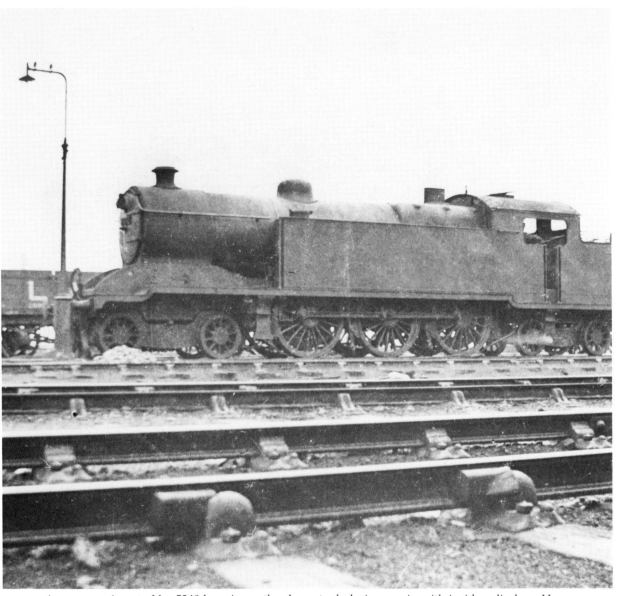

As a comparison to No. 5340 here is another large tank design, again with inside cylinders. Here LMS No. 11100, formerly a Furness Railway engine to the design of Rutherford, is included to show how different companies operated similarly styled machines around the same period.

Returning again to LNER motive power and another former Great Central design, 'C13' No. E7403 at Gorton in 1949. The 'E' prefix was a short-lived addition to the numbers of various engines prior to renumbering by BR. Certainly No. E7403 looks decidedly travel-stained, although it was destined to survive until April 1955.

1949

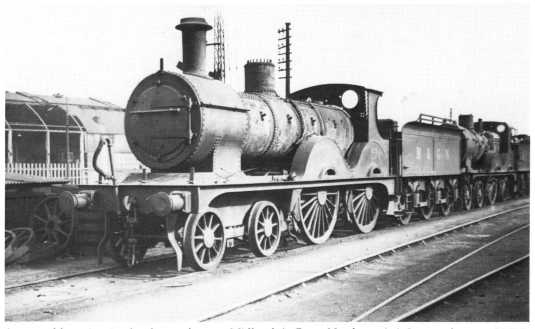

A very old engine in the form of an ex-Midland & Great Northern 4–4–0, seen here as LNER No. 043 at Stratford in 1937. Intended for passenger work on the former M&GN system, the 'Johnson' class had an interesting history, being basically an ex-Midland design, although most were built by Sharp Stewart. Despite its forlorn appearance No. 043 survived in capital stock until June 1943.

1937

Another M&GN locomotive, of the same class, this time No. 03 and again at Stratford. The former Midland Railway had been responsible for locomotive matters on the joint system – hence the continuation of their designs seen here in striking Derby style. This particular machine was withdrawn in June 1937 shortly after the photograph was taken.

May 1937

'Hunt' class depending on the name carried by a particular locomotive. All had 6 ft 8 in driving wheels and were provided with three cylinders driven by either Walschaerts valve gear or Lentz poppet valves. No. 277 *Berwickshire* is pictured at Heaton sometime between May and August 1936.

Summer 1936

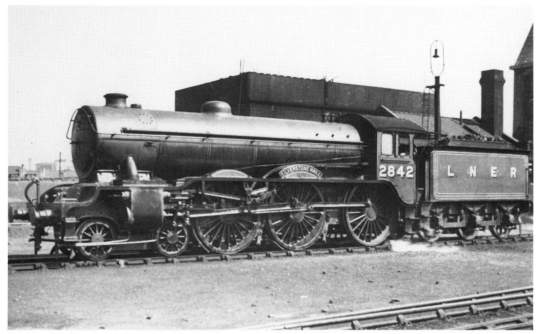

Affectionately known as the 'Sandringham' class this 4–6–0 design, introduced between 1928 and 1937, mainly worked on the former Great Eastern section of the LNER where they performed valuable service until ousted by the 'Britannia' class in BR days. No. 2842 *Kilverstone Hall* is seen at Neasden depot in early 1935.

1935

No the crane is not a permanent addition to the smoke-box! 4–4–0 No. 282 *Hurworth* at Peterborough. Compared with the previous view of No. 277, it can be seen that this engine is fitted with poppet valves.

'K3' class 2–6–0 No. 227 at Doncaster seen with some additional pipework, the purpose of which is not known. Nearly two hundred of this class were built based on a similar, but earlier, Great Northern Railway design.

A former North British Railway design 'Atlantic', No. 9905 *Buccleuch* at Carlisle. Notice that the destination 'Carlisle' is also carried on a curved board mounted above the buffer beam. Classified by the LNER as 'C10/11', the twenty-two engines of this type were taken out of service between 1933 and 1939.

1936

Although out of sequence from the intended time scale of this book, I could not resist the inclusion of this superb view of LNER No. 1699 at Rugby Locomotive Testing Station in 1949. Originally classified North Eastern Railway 'S' class, it became LNER 'B13' class and from 1934 to 1951 was used as a counter-pressure test engine.

1949

Ex-Great Eastern 'Y65', LNER 'F7' class 2–4–2T at Neasden in 1927. Nicknamed 'Crystal Palace' engines because of their cabs, these machines were the smallest of this type of engine with the 2–4–2T wheel arrangement used on the GER. Introduced in 1909/10, the twelve engines in the class were originally used on light branch duties, but later graduated to push–pull workings in the London district. Two of the class survived until 1948, having spent their final years in Scotland many miles away from their original home.

1927

Looking decidedly forlorn is former North Eastern Railway 4–6–0 No. 754 at Heaton in 1935. None of the large NER passenger classes survived on main line services with the LNER for long, such duties being taken over by the increasing number of newer Gresley engines.

1935

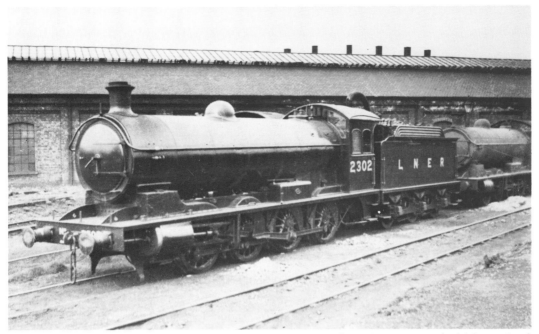

The North Eastern Railway built a number of large 0–8–0 goods engines, many of which survived beyond nationalization to almost the very end of steam on BR. Here, former NER now LNER No. 2302 at Borough Gardens and in remarkably clean external condition.

Former Great Central Railway, Robinson design 2–8–0 No. 6522 at Stratford in 1937. Large numbers of these engines saw service with the ROD overseas in the First World War and were later distributed among a variety of owners both here and abroad.

1937

North British Railway design 0–6–0 dock tank, No. 9237 at Eastfield. The use of dumb buffers will again be noted. Those were introduced to reduce the potential problems with buffer lock which might otherwise occur on some of the sharp curves on which the engine would be required to work.

Former North British Railway 0–4–0ST, seen here as LNER No. 10089 at Edinburgh, St Margarets. Fitted with dumb buffers for shunting in sharply curved yards and wharves, a number of the class were permanently attached to small wooden tenders. Despite their age – they were introduced back in 1882 – no less than thirty-three passed to BR, with the last not being withdrawn until 1963.
August 1939

Two more former GER locomotives, the first No. 8082, a larger 2–4–2T than that previously illustrated and to the former GER 'C32' class design – LNER 'F3'. Behind is what appears to be an 0–6–0T Great Eastern 'T18' class – LNER 'J66'.

Although into BR days, I could not resist the inclusion of this delightful view of E8619 on an RCTS special at North Woolwich. One of the 'J69' class, these diminutive tank engines were part of the mainstay of the steam suburban services from Liverpool Street until electrification in the early 1960s.

1951

Also recorded north of the border, although this time at Dundee in 1939, was 0–6–0T No. 9799. There is evidence of either recent welding or a slide swipe on the tank side.

Former GER 'E22' class, now LNER 'J65' No. 7253 at Stratford in 1938. Intended for light branch duties, this small 0–6–0T was designated by J.S. Holden and was first introduced in 1889. Withdrawals commenced in 1930, leaving a number of the class to spend their last years as 2–4–0Ts. They had their leading side rods removed to facilitate shunting on sharp curves.

1938

The 0–6–0T classes of 'J69' (and derivatives) were mainly employed on branch and suburban duties. Engines of this type were the last to work the steam-hauled suburban trains from Liverpool Street prior to electrification in the early 1960s. Here LNER No. 7167 is seen in a somewhat grimy external condition.

1938

Another 0–6–0T, this time No. 7340 also at Stratford in 1938.

1938

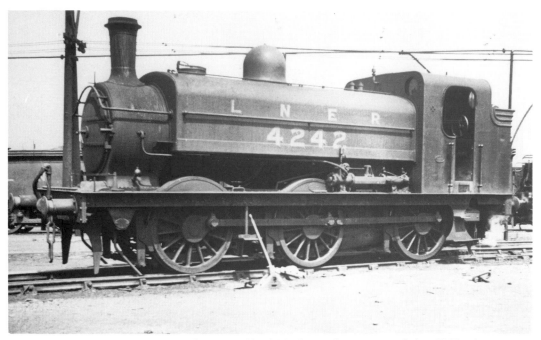

Dating from the time when Gresley was Chief Mechanical Engineer of the GNR, this is 'J22' No. 4242 at Doncaster Works in 1937.

1937

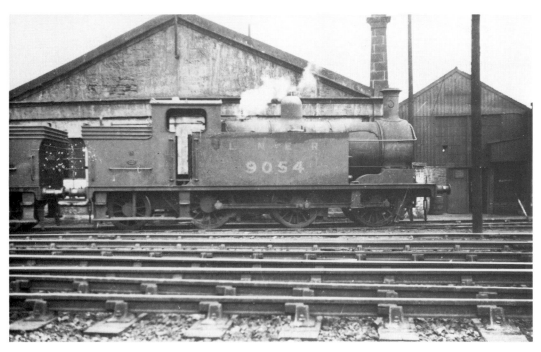

LNER No. 9054 outside Edinburgh, St Margarets.

5.8.39

Former Hull & Barnsley Railway 0–6–2T No. 2532 at Doncaster Shed. Nine of the class were built by Kitson & Co. in 1908, although all, apart from No. 2532, had been withdrawn by 1939. The engine shown was renumbered 8365 by the LNER in 1946 and was classified as being part of their 'N12' class. It was finally withdrawn in January 1949.

LNER class 'J62', an 0–6–0ST of Great Central origin and dating back to 1897. Three of the class survived into BR ownership, although all had gone by 1951. Here No. 5884 is seen at Doncaster Works complete with spark arrestor chimney.

26.6.37

Another dumb-buffered engine, No. 9237 of class 'J88'. This was a former North British Railway design and intended as a dock-tank; not all members of this class had dumb buffers as illustrated here. The class survived intact until 1954 and all were gone by 1962.

The Robinson (GCR) design of 0–6–0T, seen here as LNER No. 5157 at Brunswick. This was the side tank version of the 'J62' class previously illustrated, but designated here as 'J63'.

Developed by Gresley from the earlier, and similar, Ivatt design of 0–6–2T, this is the 'N2' class intended for suburban passenger work. No. 2683 was one of a number of the class fitted with condensing apparatus and a shorter chimney for working on the widened Metropolitan lines. It is viewed here at Kings Cross in 1936.

1936

With its characteristic Great Central design smoke-box door, this is No. 5727 of the former GCR class '3' 2–4–2T type, although it is seen here in store at Neasden in 1937. The class of twelve engines first appeared in 1892 as GCR No. 727, but did not receive the present identification until February 1925. It was withdrawn in October 1939.

1937

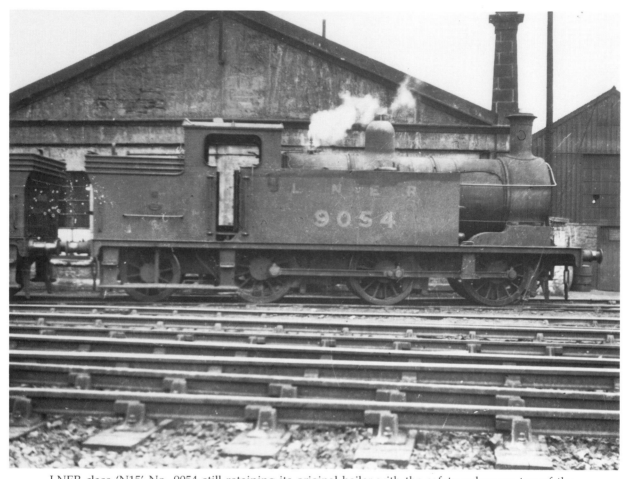

LNER class 'N15' No. 9054 still retaining its original boiler with the safety valves on top of the dome. Coming from the North British Railway, the class was a development of the earlier 'N14' class and like their earlier sisters some spent their lives as bankers on the Cowlairs incline. No. 9054, though, is seen at Edinburgh, St Margarets.

1939

From the Great Northern to the North Eastern Railway, represented here by 4–4–0 No. 676 at Darlington. The NER possessed a number of 4–4–0 engines of a similar style, which, despite their appearance in the photograph, were striking machines when wearing the spotless livery of earlier years.

Starting off life as a 2–4–0 passenger engine, a number of the Great Eastern 'T19' class were rebuilt as 4–4–0s and used on a variety of passenger duties. Photographed in store at Stratford in 1938, is LNER No. 8029.

1938

Far from its normal haunts, is former GCR 0–6–0 No. 5090 at Chester in 1935.

1935

North British Railway 0–6–0, now LNER 'J36' No. 9301 at Heaton. Between 1888 and 1900 one hundred and sixty-eight engines of this class were built, with twenty-five serving in France during the First World War.

LNER 'J50' class 0–6–0T No. 2792 in smart black livery at Doncaster Works. This class of locomotive was a development of a similar Great Northern design, one hundred and two of which passed into BR hands.

1937

Appropriately referred to as the 'Scott' class, this is former NBR 4–4–0 *Sir Walter Scott* is seen here as LNER No. 9898 at Carlisle. As with a number of other companies who had their own style for a particular feature of locomotive design, NER machines were recognizable by the additional handrail on the top half of the smoke-box door.

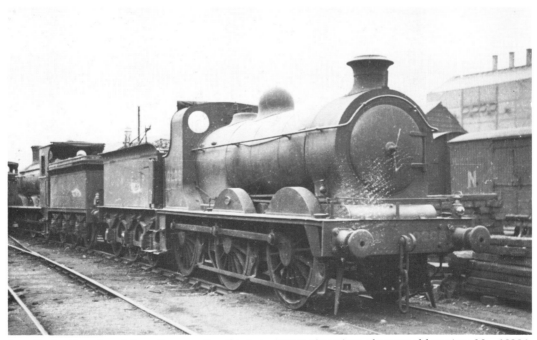

Despite the thumb print on the negative this is an interesting view of a very old engine, No. 10206. Notice the spartan protection for the crew and also the basic three-link coupling at the front.

1935

Another early 0–6–0, this one is believed to be of GNR origin. LNER No. 9249 photographed at what is stated to be 'Kipps'.

1935

War Department 0–6–0 No. 75028 depicted at Longmoor, Hampshire. A number of these 0–6–0 design engines later passed to the LNER and BR (E) as class 'J94', while an even larger quantity were sold for use in outside industry.

1941

Variety at Selby, with 0–6–0 No. 2515 parked by a spare tender and one of the Sentinel steam rail-cars behind.

Approaching the conclusion of the LNER section I could not resist another view of a former M&GN 0–6–0, represented here by No. 059 at Stratford in 1937 and in reasonable external condition.

1937

Riddles design, War Department, 2–8–0 No. 77473 at Bricklayers Arms, Southern Railway. A number of this design, including this particular machine, were later purchased by the LNER. No. 77473 became LNER 3112; it was subsequently renumbered again as BR No. 90433 and lasted in service until April 1964.

Miscellaneous Railways

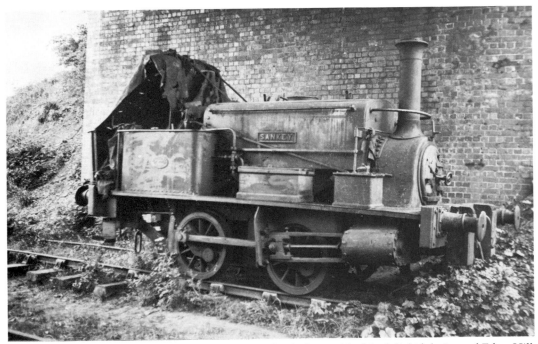

What better way to start the final section of the book than with this delightful view of Edge Hill Railway 0–4–0 *Sankey*, derelict and out of use. Little else is known of either the locomotive or the railway on which it worked, although I presume it to have been in the Liverpool area.

24.6.39

Metropolitan 0–4–0T No. 80 on a Chesham
branch train.

1938

With funnel missing, Jersey Railway *St Aubins* on a passenger train. The presence of a jack on the framing was perhaps somewhat optimistic as it would have been unlikely that the crew could have effected a re-railing exercise on their own should it have been necessary.

c. 1938

Bedecked in striking maroon livery, this is Metropolitan No. 101 at Neasden depot where it spent much of its time on shunting duties. In the background part of the power station can be seen.

Another Metropolitan machine, this time 0–6–4T No. 96, being prepared for duty at Neasden.

At the same time as recording the contemporary scene in England, Scotland and Wales, Bernard Anwell also visited Ireland. He took photographs at three locations, although, regretfully reporting only the briefest of details. Accordingly, information on the steam engines themselves is somewhat sketchy. Even so they are worthy of inclusion. Here the first Great Southern Railway, No. 537 is seen at Dublin Broadstone.

July 1939

The same location and 0–6–0 No. 622, another engine originating from the GSR. The extended smoke box and outside cabling spoils the otherwise neat lines of the machine, although judging from the similar engine reposing inside the shed such additions were by no means uncommon.

One of the large Metropolitan 2–6–4T designs, which bore a remarkable similarity to contemporary Southern Railway machines. No. 115 displaying the typically clean appearance of this railway's steam engines.

Moving north now to Belfast, and Belfast & County Down Railway 4–4–2T No. 19 is seen attached to a passenger vehicle or van. With a limited network of lines and none really suitable for the high speeds then being attained in England, a number of these smaller and older machines survived on the Irish system for some years.

Returning to Broadstone and a view of GSR No. 614. Ireland was the starting place for the career of several mechanical engineers who later achieved fame in England. Perhaps the best known of these was R.E.L. Maunsell. Conversely there was also a move by at least one man in the opposite direction, ironically Maunsell's successor on the SR. This was Bulleid who, having failed with his 'Leader' design on the SR, attempted a similar project in Ireland. For different reasons this too was destined to failure.

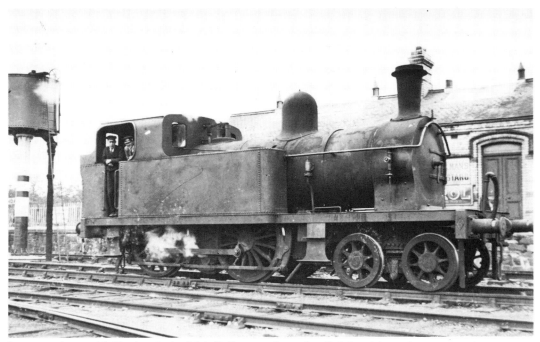

In comparison with England, the Irish Railways adopted a slightly wider rail gauge at 5 ft 3 in. This is apparent from the photograph from the mixture of flat bottom and bull-head rail. Seen at Dundalk is Great Northern design 4–4–0T No. 195.

July 1939

Concluding the sequence is a former 0–6–0 evidently in the process of being slowly dismembered. Former GSR No. 475 stands silently at Dublin Broadstone and, although minus the centre pair of driving wheels, still retains a cast numberplate – the days before the souvenier hunter!